The Book that Everyone Should Have

The most important guide you could share with the ones you love

IRA STARR

Printed in the United States of America.
Library of Congress Control Number: 2019937889
ISBN: 978-1-949639-44-5

Book Design & Illustrations: Clara Starr

This Book Belongs To:

About the Author

Since 1985, Ira Starr, MRFC, LUTCF® has been providing holistic based financial planning guidance to individuals, families, estate administrators, and entrepreneurial business owners.

Starr graduated from the University of Maryland, having studied economics, finance, psychology and completed one of the first personal finance courses offered at the university level.

Starr received the NCCA accredited credential of Master Registered Financial Consultant from the certification board of the International Association of Registered Financial Consultants. Upon satisfying the educational, ethical, and experience requirements established by the board of trustees of the American College and National Association of Insurance and Financial Advisors (NAIFA), Starr received the LUTCF® designation.

Starr is a sought-out mentor to financial advisors across the country, participates on financial educational panels, and has published articles in multiple financial organization trade journals. He is also a member of several independent industry trade groups that focus on enhancing public financial understanding and well-being through education.

Starr has served on boards of directors for both private and charter public schools, and as of this writing serves on the board of a global non-profit educational institution. In addition, he is a president's advisory board member for an organization specializing in training financial advisors to communicate complex personal financial, estate, and retirement concepts in a simple and understandable fashion.

Starr is a certified member of the International Association of Registered Financial Consultants and the National Ethics Association.

Starr is happily married and the proud father of three children, and he lives in the Asheville area of North Carolina where he enjoys various outdoor activities, his two horses, and his blue heeler dog.

Introduction

When you picked up this book, you most likely asked yourself: "The book that *everyone* should have? Everyone, really?"

The answer? "Yes!" The book you have in your hands is more than a simple self-help book; it is a book that will guide you and your loved ones through financial planning for the major changes one might experience in life, such as incapacity, marriage, divorce, death, or natural/other disaster.

Some people might resist reading this book because even just thinking about catastrophic or monumental life changes is uncomfortable and stressful. Those events represent huge and mysterious changes that people either can't or won't wrap their heads around. In reality, these kinds of things happen to people every day, and, inevitably, someone you love and care about—maybe even you—will have to figure out how to pick up the pieces.

Deep down we all know that avoidance isn't a real solution. No matter what your situation is, no matter how much or how little wealth you have, no matter how beautifully your family gets along, collecting your information in this book will radically improve your and your loved ones' situation. This could mean having an easier time planning your day-to-day financial affairs, or handling a major life-changing event (such as the birth of a child/grandchild), or even recovering your information after a natural disaster. Or it could mean, in case of your own incapacity or passing away, helping your heirs locate your information and understand all your wishes. Whatever change comes, you will be glad you picked up this book and completed it in advance.

Many people have their whole financial lives scattered across different accounts, junk drawers, notebooks and in online file folders. Consolidating your information in this one slim volume will help you map out your wishes and intentions with regard to your health, your wealth, and anything else that someone may need to know when you aren't available for consultation. No one should have to run around to a dozen different places to find this kind of information, and, should you complete this book, you won't have to—you'll have what amounts to an owner's manual for your life that you or the people you choose can access whenever it's needed.

The personal nature of these decisions were a big part of the reason to create a physical book, rather than some sort of website, database, or app. You can, of course, record your information digitally (in fact, I encourage people to have multiple copies of their information available). But, evidence suggests that the act of writing information down actually makes us more likely to remember that information, not to mention that there's something personal and intimate about the act of writing.[1] When you look back on a book you've filled in by hand, there's a sense of ownership that doesn't necessarily come with entering data into a computer.

Having a physical record of your information is also important from a security standpoint. Many people feel they don't need to collect all their information because they believe they "have it all online somewhere." But how do our loved ones access our information if we are unable to give them all those usernames and passcodes? In addition, we live in an age of data trafficking where your informa-

---

1   Lizette Borreli, "Why Using Pen And Paper, Not Laptops, Boosts Memory: Writing Notes Helps Recall Concepts, Ability To Understand," Medical Daily, February 6, 2014, https://www.medicaldaily.com/why-using-pen-and-paper-not-laptops-boosts-memory-writing-notes-helps-recall-concepts-ability-268770.

tion is one of the most valuable commodities online. Breaches, hacks, software and server failures—all of these are regular parts of our lives now, as well as major retail companies losing customer information, banking institutions creating fake accounts, and other informational databases being shockingly vulnerable. A book, of course, has vulnerabilities too, but you won't ever have to worry that a glitch in the cloud is going to make it disappear.

The book is also intended to be a living document—you can revisit it whenever something about your life or situation changes. Adding new information or amending old entries is easy and simple. Above all else, the book is designed to be straightforward and accessible to everyone. If you spend a few minutes a day on your book, you should be able to complete your book in a week or so, and the "upkeep" required at that point will be just a few more minutes whenever you make a major change. So, take ten minutes here and there, record your information and organize your wishes, keep the book in a safe place, and let the people you love know the location of the book. Lift the burden from their shoulders and lift the apprehension from yours.

People who seemingly have every reason in the world to carefully plan for major life changes have resisted putting even simple structures in place. Audrey Hepburn, John Denver, Pablo Picasso, Marlon Brando, Aretha Franklin, Prince, Robert Brooks, Gary Coleman, Steve McNair, Dennis Hopper, Alan Thicke, Muhammed Ali, B.B. King … all of these were famous, accomplished people with large, complicated financial assets, and some of them left little or nothing in the way of direction for their heirs or estate managers. If they realized that their vast and complicated holdings could result in struggle and strife, they probably would have seen to hiring a fleet of people to design wills, trusts, and advanced directives. They, themselves, could have journaled a simple guide providing direction and clarity to their loved ones. But they didn't fully plan for any of it. And it wasn't because some were caught unaware, either—Pablo Picasso was ninety-one when he died, while Audrey Hepburn and Aretha Franklin were both well aware that they had terminal illnesses long before their deaths. For example, John Denver, who famously died young in a plane crash, and Prince, who died at fifty-seven of an accidental overdose, could really be said to have lacked the time to get their affairs in order. Even still, they were successful musicians for years and could surely see that their holdings and assets were becoming more intricate and complex by the day.

Whether you're a billionaire or are living paycheck to paycheck, we are all united by certain human experiences involving dramatic change. Unfortunately, no amount of money, fame, or assistance can keep those changes from touching our lives. Preparing for life events means we can spare our loved ones the work on top of the heartbreak and shock that goes hand-in-hand with those life changing events.

There are numerous reasons people tend to avoid this kind of planning, and there are many ways inaction can end up hurting the people they love. For example, maybe you think your family is so rock-solid that they'd never fight over something as relatively "unimportant" as money. Perhaps you don't have much in the way of assets and don't think you need to spend time organizing what little you have, or maybe you simply assume that it can't be that complicated and that there's probably some system in place that will work everything out. Maybe you truly believe that you've already taken care of anything that could possibly come up.

If that's the case, here are a few stories from real-life situations (the names of the people featured are fictional) to illustrate what could happen without written plans in place.

The Artist

Thomas Larsen was a brilliant creative mind, a true once-in-a-generation talent. His work is taught in universities and fetches millions at auction. That same work will live on long after his death and will remain highly valuable, which presents a unique challenge for his estate.

His estate isn't short on challenges to begin with. A complicated man, Larsen had a somewhat messy personal life and he has no fewer than seventeen potential heirs, including ex-wives, long-time mistresses, children (legitimate and otherwise), protégées, and other assorted people to whom he'd promised some nebulous "share" of his vast wealth.

Before Larsen was even in the ground, everyone who could afford to hired a lawyer, and a prolonged battle royale began. It stretched on and on (… and on and on) while legal fees and taxes slowly ate up the bulk of the remaining wealth. By the time the many litigants managed to come to an agreement, there was little left but pocket change. And, for everyone involved, warm memories of the man himself had been replaced by bitter reminisces about the years and dollars wasted.

The Good Mother

Gloria Barrett spent her life just scraping by. Her greatest source of pride was having successfully raised two daughters on her own while working a series of blue-collar jobs. Always focused on getting through until the next paycheck, Gloria rarely thought about estate planning because she figured she had no "estate" to plan.

What she didn't anticipate—what no one could have anticipated—was the sudden stroke that left her unable to communicate or care for herself. Only sixty-five and in otherwise good health, Gloria needed extensive and expensive care for years to come. Without any guidance from Gloria, her daughters were left to make all the medical and legal decisions themselves.

It wasn't long before the stress of the situation took a toll on the daughters. The younger one began to resent how she came to shoulder most of the day-to-day responsibility for their mother. Her older sister, meanwhile, worried that the younger sister wasn't making the most sensible decisions and wanted more control over the process. Both of them regularly wished Mom could simply tell them what she wanted.

The Whiz Kid

Jordan Emerson grew up on the internet and he completely embraced the freedom and versatility that living a digital life offered to him. A freelancer, he moved frequently and relied upon online services to keep him connected, whether he was in Hong Kong or Houston. He lived an almost paperless lifestyle, paying for everything from his lunch to his health insurance bill with a collection of apps. And, in possibly the biggest mistake of his life, he used a password manager to generate unique, impossible-to-crack passwords for all of his accounts.

When that password manager's parent company was hacked, releasing the data of millions of users, Jordan suddenly found himself exposed. Not all of his accounts were impacted, but enough were that he soon found himself spending entire days on the phone struggling to prove that he was himself with half-remembered security questions and the few paper documents he could find at his parents' place. It was years before he was able to regain full control of his accounts and, even then, he still had to carefully monitor his credit reports for irregularities. More than anything else, Jordan felt the loss of the freedom and security he had felt before the breach.

The Favorite

Jerome McCormick was besotted with his first grandbaby, and, as soon as he set eyes on the boy, he knew he wanted to do something to protect and insure his future. So, shortly after Sam was born, Jerome met with his financial advisor and re-allocated a significant portion of his wealth to a trust fund in the child's name.

Fast-forward seventeen years and Sam is everything a proud grandpa could hope for—salutatorian and a swimming star, he'd attend college on a full-ride sports scholarship. During those seventeen years, four more grandkids have also been added to the family, all of whom Jerome dotes upon.

Somehow, in the course of those years, Jerome forgot his structuring of that trust for Sam. If you had asked him about it, he would have said of course it wasn't fair or right to leave an inheritance to only one grandchild—especially one that already had his college funding locked in—but, unfortunately, no one asked him.

It wasn't until after Jerome's death that his family discovered the lopsided inheritance. Even the most happy-go-lucky of Jerome's grandchildren couldn't help but wonder what they had done wrong. It would have broken Jerome's heart to see his family like that, and it was never his intention to make anyone feel left out or skipped over, but that was, nevertheless, the message he sent with his estate planning documents—or rather, lack thereof.

The Free-Spirit

Ellie Getz never saw eye-to-eye with her parents. By the time she was sixteen, the relationship was so irreparably damaged that she left home, never to return. Half kicked out and half running away, Ellie nevertheless managed to make a good life for herself. She had a group of friends she loved and a job she cherished, and the best part was that she and no one else got to choose the direction of her new life.

All of that changed after a fatal car accident shortly before her twenty-first birthday. Though she hadn't seen or spoken to them in years, her parents were still her legal next-of-kin, and they immediately swooped in to take over all the arrangements. Her friends—her chosen family—were shut out completely.

It seemed like such a particular betrayal of her memory and spirit—Ellie had done everything she could to escape her parent's control only to have them wrench it all back at her death—but there was nothing her friends could do. After all, legally her parents had every right to do as they did, even though everyone who knew Ellie knew that her wishes were not being honored.

These stories illustrate how things can go awry. It all comes back to that inevitability of change—none of us can predict the future because our future is always in flux. None of the people in these stories expected or wanted the fallout that came after some catastrophic change, and they weren't bad or selfish people. Their error was not being able or willing to think through these eventualities before they happened. Because they didn't write down their wishes, intentions, and information, other people had to pick up the pieces. Sadly, failing to make their wishes clear meant those wishes went unfulfilled.

The Book that Everyone Should Have is the book that everyone needs because everyone is on a journey; no one lives a static life. Making life easier to weather twists and turns is the best, most loving gift you can give to the people around you, and also to yourself.

Once you fill out this book, it will serve as one of the greatest gestures of love for the significant others in your life. When you sit down to look through the book, don't think about obligations or to-do lists; rather, picture the faces of people you love, the people you want to provide for and protect. This could even be yourself, in a future where things have gotten messy or even frightening.

As you go through the book, think of your loved ones and imagine you are writing them a letter they will read in a time of turmoil. Think of what they will want to hear, the information they will need to have to make things simple, and then give them all those things. What a great privilege to provide those you love with knowledge and security. What a blessing for you to make life easier and more peaceful for them.

People Who Know About this Book

My Personal Information

Legal Name:

Maiden Name:

Address:

PO Box:

Location of PO Box Key:

Cell Phone #:

Home Phone #:

Business Phone #:

Social Security #:

Birthplace:

Citizenship:

Marital Status:

Spouse/Significant Other's Name:

Children's Names (natural/other):

Grandchildren's Names:

Sibling's Names:

Father's Name:

Father's Birthplace:

Mother's Name:

Mother's Maiden Name:

Mother's Birthplace:

Maternal Extended Family (note relationship of each):

Paternal Extended Family (note relationship of each):

Names of Closest Friends:

My Medical Information

Blood Type:

Medications:

Allergies & Reactions:

Primary Care Doctor:

Phone #:

Address:

Preferred Hospital:

Phone #:

Address:

Preferred Pharmacy:

Phone #:

Address:

Health Plan:

Health Plan Card #:

Phone #:

Dental Plan:

Dental Plan Card #:

Phone #:

Vision Plan:

Vision Plan Card #:

Phone #:

Prescription Plan:

Prescription Plan Card #:

Phone #:

Location of Living Will:

Location of Healthcare Power of Attorney:

Location of Organ Donation/Anatomical Gift Information:

Appointed Agent:

Phone #:

Address:

Successor Appointed Agent:

Phone #:

Address:

If I Am Unable to Communicate

For My Caregiver to Know:

Essential Financial & Estate Contact Information

Personal Representative (Executor):

Phone #:

Address:

Joint and/or Successor Personal Representative:

Phone #:

Address:

Successor Trustee for Existing Living Trust:

Phone #:

Address:

Trustee for Testamentary Trust:

Phone #:

Address:

Successor Trustee for Testamentary Trust:

Phone #:

Address:

Guardian for Minor Child/Children:

Phone #:

Address:

Successor Guardian:

Phone #:

Address:

Attorney:

Phone #:

Address:

Accountant:

Phone #:

Address:

Financial Advisor:

Phone #:

Address:

At the Time of My Passing

Please request 10 copies of my death certificate for
estate settlement purposes, a service usually
provided by your funeral contact.

PLEASE CONTACT THE FOLLOWING

Religious/Spiritual Advisor:

Phone #:

Address:

Family Member:

Phone #:

Address:

Family Member:

Phone #:

Address:

Family Member:

Phone #:

Address:

Family Member:

Phone #:

Address:

Family Member:

Phone #:

Address:

Family Member:

Phone #:

Address:

Family Member:

Phone #:

Address:

Family Member:

Phone #:

Address:

Family Member:

Phone #:

Address:

Family Member:

Phone #:

Address:

Family Member:

Phone #:

Address:

Family Member:

Phone #:

Address:

Family Member:

Phone #:

Address:

Friend:

Phone #:

Address:

Friend:

Phone #:

Address:

Friend:

Phone #:

Address:

Friend:

Phone #:

Address:

Friend:

Phone #:

Address:

Friend:

Phone #:

Address:

Friend:

Phone #:

Address:

Friend:

Phone #:

Address:

Friend:

Phone #:

Address:

Friend:

Phone #:

Address:

Final Arrangements & Personal Wishes

Prearranged Funeral Paperwork Location:

Final Expense Insurance Policy #:

Company Name:

Phone #:

Funeral Home:

Phone #:

Address:

Instructions For My Remains:

Burial:

Name of Cemetery:

Address:

Memorial Stone:

Cremation:

Special Instructions for Ashes:

Other Personal Wishes, Desired Arrangements and Military Honors:

Information To Be Included in Obituary:

Disability & Long Term Care Insurance

If Short/Long Term Disability Benefit is offered through employer
contact employer/human resources department for policy information

Personal Long Term Disability Insurance Policy #:

Agent Name:

Phone #:

Company Name:

Phone #:

Address:

Long Term Care Policy #:

Agent Name:

Company Name:

Phone #:

Address:

Long Term Care Preferences (carehome, etc.):

My Dependents

Children, Aging Parents,
Or Friends Dependent On Me

Name:

Phone #:

Address:

Birthdate & Birthplace: Citizenship:

Relationship:

Special Considerations:

Name:

Phone #:

Address:

Birthdate & Birthplace: Citizenship:

Relationship:

Special Considerations:

Name:

Phone #:

Address:

Birthdate & Birthplace: Citizenship:

Relationship:

Special Considerations:

Name:

Phone #:

Address:

Birthdate & Birthplace: Citizenship:

Relationship:

Special Considerations:

Name:

Phone #:

Address:

Birthdate & Birthplace: Citizenship:

Relationship:

Special Considerations:

Name:

Phone #:

Address:

Birthdate & Birthplace: Citizenship:

Relationship:

Special Considerations:

Name:

Phone #:

Address:

Birthdate & Birthplace: Citizenship:

Relationship:

Special Considerations:

Name:

Phone #:

Address:

Birthdate & Birthplace: Citizenship:

Relationship:

Special Considerations:

Important Documents

Location & Date of Last Will:

Driver's License #:

Passport #:

Date of Issue:

Date of Expiration:

Location of Passport:

Location of Birth Certificate:

Location of Marriage Certificate:

Location of Divorce Decree:

Location of Military Discharge Papers:

Location of My Contact/Address Book:

Financial Information

Location of Financial/General Durable Power of Attorney:

Date of Document:

My Appointed Agent:

Phone #:

Address:

Successor Appointed Agent:

Phone #:

Address:

TAX RECORDS

Location of Federal & State Records:

Online Tax Account:

User Name:

Password:

BANKING INFORMATION

Bank Name:

Primary Branch:

Bank Manager:

Phone #:

Address:

Checking Account #:

Savings Account #:

CD Account #:

ATM/Debit Card:

Account #:

PIN #:

ATM/Debit Card:

Account #:

PIN #:

SAFE DEPOSIT BOX

Bank Name:

Phone #:

Address:

Box #:

Location of Key:

Other Authorized Signer:

Phone #:

Address:

SECONDARY BANKING INFORMATION

Bank Name:

Primary Branch:

Bank Manager:

Phone #:

Address:

Checking Account #:

Savings Account #:

CD Account #:

ATM/Debit Card:

Account #:

PIN #:

Credit Card Information

Mastercard ☐   Visa ☐   AmEx ☐   Discover ☐   Other ☐

Account #: ___________________   Phone #: ___________________

Online User Name: _____________   Password: ___________________

Expiration Date: ______________   CV code #: __________________

Mastercard ☐   Visa ☐   AmEx ☐   Discover ☐   Other ☐

Account #: ___________________   Phone #: ___________________

Online User Name: _____________   Password: ___________________

Expiration Date: ______________   CV code #: __________________

Mastercard ☐   Visa ☐   AmEx ☐   Discover ☐   Other ☐

Account #: ___________________   Phone #: ___________________

Online User Name: _____________   Password: ___________________

Expiration Date: ______________   CV code #: __________________

Mastercard ☐   Visa ☐   AmEx ☐   Discover ☐   Other ☐

Account #: ___________________   Phone #: ___________________

Online User Name: _____________   Password: ___________________

Expiration Date: ______________   CV code #: __________________

Mastercard ☐   Visa ☐   AmEx ☐   Discover ☐   Other ☐

Account #: ______________________   Phone #: ______________________

Online User Name: ______________________   Password: ______________________

Expiration Date: ______________________   CV code #: ______________________

Mastercard ☐   Visa ☐   AmEx ☐   Discover ☐   Other ☐

Account #: ______________________   Phone #: ______________________

Online User Name: ______________________   Password: ______________________

Expiration Date: ______________________   CV code #: ______________________

Mastercard ☐   Visa ☐   AmEx ☐   Discover ☐   Other ☐

Account #: ______________________   Phone #: ______________________

Online User Name: ______________________   Password: ______________________

Expiration Date: ______________________   CV code #: ______________________

Mastercard ☐   Visa ☐   AmEx ☐   Discover ☐   Other ☐

Account #: ______________________   Phone #: ______________________

Online User Name: ______________________   Password: ______________________

Expiration Date: ______________________   CV code #: ______________________

Mastercard ☐   Visa ☐   AmEx ☐   Discover ☐   Other ☐

Account #: ___________________________   Phone #: ___________________________

Online User Name: ____________________   Password: __________________________

Expiration Date: ______________________   CV code #: _________________________

Mastercard ☐   Visa ☐   AmEx ☐   Discover ☐   Other ☐

Account #: ___________________________   Phone #: ___________________________

Online User Name: ____________________   Password: __________________________

Expiration Date: ______________________   CV code #: _________________________

Mastercard ☐   Visa ☐   AmEx ☐   Discover ☐   Other ☐

Account #: ___________________________   Phone #: ___________________________

Online User Name: ____________________   Password: __________________________

Expiration Date: ______________________   CV code #: _________________________

Mastercard ☐   Visa ☐   AmEx ☐   Discover ☐   Other ☐

Account #: ___________________________   Phone #: ___________________________

Online User Name: ____________________   Password: __________________________

Expiration Date: ______________________   CV code #: _________________________

Investment Brokerage Accounts

Firm Name:

Type of Account:

Account #:

Phone #:

Address:

Online User Name:

Password:

Secondary Access Verification Answer:

Firm Name:

Type of Account:

Account #:

Phone #:

Address:

Online User Name:

Password:

Secondary Access Verification Answer:

Firm Name:

Type of Account:

Account #:

Phone #:

Address:

Online User Name:

Password:

Secondary Access Verification Answer:

Firm Name:

Type of Account:

Account #:

Phone #:

Address:

Online User Name:

Password:

Secondary Access Verification Answer:

Firm Name:

Type of Account:

Account #:

Phone #:

Address:

Online User Name:

Password:

Secondary Access Verification Answer:

Firm Name:

Type of Account:

Account #:

Phone #:

Address:

Online User Name:

Password:

Secondary Access Verification Answer:

Frequent Flyer Rewards Programs, Etc.

Name of Account:

Account #:   Phone #:

Online User Name: Password:

Name of Account:

Account #:   Phone #:

Online User Name: Password:

Name of Account:

Account #:   Phone #:

Online User Name: Password:

Name of Account:

Account #:   Phone #:

Online User Name: Password:

Name of Account:

Account #:   Phone #:

Online User Name: Password:

Personal Liabilities

Primary Mortgage:

Servicing Lender Name:

Account #:

Online Access Name:

Password:

Phone #:

Location of Closing Documents/Deed, etc.:

Secondary Mortgage:

Servicing Lender Name:

Account #:

Online Access Name:

Password:

Phone #:

Location of Closing Documents/Deed, etc.:

Home Equity Line of Credit (HELOC): _______________________________

Bank Name: _______________________________

Address: _______________________________

____

Account #: _______________________________

Online Access Name: _______________________________

Password: _______________________________

Phone #: _______________________________

Location of Closing Documents/Deed, etc.: _______________________________

____

Car Loan: _______________________________

Lender Name: _______________________________

Address: _______________________________

____

Account #: _______________________________

Online Access Name: _______________________________

Password: _______________________________

Phone #: _______________________________

Location of Title: _______________________________

____

____

Car Loan:

Lender Name:

Address:

Account #:

Online Access Name:

Password:

Phone #:

Location of Title:

Student Loan:

Lender Name:

Account #:

Lender Phone #:

Location of Papers:

Student Loan:

Lender Name:

Account #:

Lender Phone #:

Location of Papers:

Medical Bills:

Contact Information:

Account #:

Location of Papers:

Personal Line of Credit:

Bank/Institution Name:

Address:

Phone #:

Account #:

Location of Papers:

Private/Personal Loans:

Name of Lender:

Address:

Phone #:

Account #:

Location of Papers:

Business Related Loans:

Lender Name:

Address:

Account #:

Location of Papers/Other Information:

Business Related Loans:

Lender Name:

Address:

Account #:

Location of Papers/Other Information:

What is Owed to Me

Personal Loans:

Contact Information:

Details:

Location of Papers:

Personal Loans:

Contact Information:

Details:

Location of Papers:

Possessions:

Contact Information:

Details:

Location of Papers:

Other:

Contact Information:

Details:

Location of Papers:

LIFE INSURANCE POLICIES

Type of Policy:

Policy #:

Company Name:

Phone #:

Agent Name:

Phone #:

Amount:

Beneficiary List & Policy Location:

Type of Policy:

Policy #:

Company Name:

Phone #:

Agent Name:

Phone #:

Amount:

Beneficiary List & Policy Location:

Type of Policy:

Policy #:

Company Name:

Phone #:

Agent Name:

Phone #:

Amount:

Beneficiary List & Policy Location:

Type of Policy:

Policy #:

Company Name:

Phone #:

Agent Name:

Phone #:

Amount:

Beneficiary List & Policy Location:

EMPLOYER BENEFITS

Name of Employer:

Benefit Administrator:

Phone #:

Retirement Savings Account #:

Location of Benefit Paperwork:

SOCIAL SECURITY

Online Login Information:

Local Branch Office Address:

Location of Benefit Statement:

VETERAN BENEFITS

Local VA Office:

Phone #:

Address:

Location of Military Service Documents:

PERSONAL QUALIFIED RETIREMENT ACCOUNTS (IRAs, etc.)

BANK

Bank Name:

Branch:

Phone #:

Account #:

Beneficiary List & Document Location:

Bank Name:

Branch:

Phone #:

Account #:

Beneficiary List & Document Location:

BROKERAGE

Company:

Phone #:

Account #:

Beneficiary List & Document Location:

ANNUITIES

Company:

Phone #:

Account #:

Beneficiary List & Document Location:

Company:

Phone #:

Account #:

Beneficiary List & Document Location:

Company:

Phone #:

Account #:

Beneficiary List & Document Location:

Company:

Phone #:

Account #:

Beneficiary List & Document Location:

SELF DIRECTED IRA

Company:

Phone #:

Account #:

Beneficiary List & Document Location:

ADDITIONAL ACCOUNTS

REAL ESTATE

Primary Residence:

Address:

Co-owner:

Location of Legal Documents:

Home Owner's Insurance Policy #:

Company Name:

Phone #:

Location of Spare Keys:

Location of Warranties:

Home Security Company Name:

Phone #:

Account #:

Home Security Access Code:

Secondary Residence:

Address:

Co-owner:

Location of Legal Documents:

Home Owner's Insurance Policy #:

Company Name:

Phone #:

Location of Spare Keys:

Location of Warranties:

Home Security Company Contact:

Home Security Access Code:

Raw Land:

Address:

Co-owner:

Location of Legal Documents:

Property Insurance Policy #:

Company Name:

Phone #:

Rental Property 1:

Address:

Location of Current Lease Agreement:

Management Company:

Phone #:

Property Insurance Policy #:

Company Name:

Phone #:

Location of Spare Keys:

Rental Property 2:

Address:

Location of Current Lease Agreement:

Management Company:

Phone #:

Property Insurance Policy #:

Company Name:

Phone #:

Location of Spare Keys:

Commercial Property:

Address:

Co-owner Name:

Phone #:

Location of Legal Documents:

Location of Spare Keys:

VEHICLES (CARS, TRUCKS, MOTORBIKES, RV'S, ETC.)

Vehicle:

Year/Make/Model/Color:

VIN/ID:

Location of Title:

Location of Lease/Loan Information:

Location of Spare Keys:

Vehicle Insurance Policy #:

Company Name:

Phone #:

Vehicle:

Year/Make/Model/Color:

VIN/ID:

Location of Title:

Location of Lease/Loan Information:

Location of Spare Keys:

Vehicle Insurance Policy #:

Company Name:

Phone #:

Vehicle: ____

Year/Make/Model/Color: _______________________________

VIN/ID: ____

Location of Title: _____________________________________

Location of Lease/Loan Information: ____________________

Location of Spare Keys: ________________________________

Vehicle Insurance Policy #: ____________________________

Company Name: ____

Phone #: ____

____

Vehicle: ____

Year/Make/Model/Color: _______________________________

VIN/ID: ____

Location of Title: _____________________________________

Location of Lease/Loan Information: ____________________

Location of Spare Keys: ________________________________

Vehicle Insurance Policy #: ____________________________

Company Name: ____

Phone #: ____

SPECIAL HEIRLOOMS

Item:

Location:

Instructions:

Item:

Location:

Instructions:

Item:

Location:

Instructions:

Item:

Location:

Instructions:

Item:

Location:

Instructions:

Item:

Location:

Instructions:

Item:

Location:

Instructions:

Item:

Location:

Instructions:

Item:

Location:

Instructions:

Item:

Location:

Instructions:

Item:

Location:

Instructions:

Item:

Location:

Instructions:

Item:

Location:

Instructions:

Item:

Location:

Instructions:

Item:

Location:

Instructions:

Item:

Location:

Instructions:

Item:

Location:

Instructions:

Item:

Location:

Instructions:

Item:

Location:

Instructions:

Item:

Location:

Instructions:

FIREARMS

Location:

Description & Registration Information:

Permit Information:

STORAGE UNIT

Name of Facility:

Address:

Phone #:

Facility Access Code #:

Unit #:

Location of Spare Keys:

Combination Lock #:

Storage Unit Policy Company:

Storage Unit Policy #:

Phone #:

SAFE

Location:

Location of Spare Keys:

Combination Lock #:

Pets

Pet Name:

Age/Description:

Veterinarian:

Phone #:

Person Who Will Take Care of Pet:

Name:

Phone #:

Instructions:

Pet Name:

Age/Description:

Veterinarian:

Phone #:

Person Who Will Take Care of Pet:

Name:

Phone #:

Instructions:

Pet Name:

Age/Description:

Veterinarian:

Phone #:

Person Who Will Take Care of Pet:

Name:

Phone #:

Instructions:

Pet Name:

Age/Description:

Veterinarian:

Phone #:

Person Who Will Take Care of Pet:

Name:

Phone #:

Instructions:

Pet Name:

Age/Description:

Veterinarian:

Phone #:

Person Who Will Take Care of Pet:

Name:

Phone #:

Instructions:

Pet Name:

Age/Description:

Veterinarian:

Phone #:

Person Who Will Take Care of Pet:

Name:

Phone #:

Instructions:

On-Going Bills

In Addition to Major Credit Cards from the Earlier Section

Gas & Oil Utilities:

Phone #:

Electric Utility:

Phone #:

Water Service:

Phone #:

Home Phone Provider:

Phone #:

Cell Phone Provider:

Phone #:

Cable Television/Internet Provier:

Phone #:

ONLINE CONSUMER RETAIL ACCOUNTS

Account Name:

Account #:

User Name:

Password:

Account Name:

Account #:

User Name:

Password:

Account Name:

Account #:

User Name:

Password:

Account Name:

Account #:

User Name:

Password:

CHARITIES I WISH TO SUPPORT

Charity Name:

Phone #:

Charity Name:

Phone #:

Charity Name:

Phone #:

Charity Name:

Phone #:

Charity Name:

Phone #:

Charity Name:

Phone #:

PHYSICAL & ONLINE SUBSCRIPTIONS

Publication Name:

Phone #:

Publication Name:

Phone #:

Publication Name:

Phone #:

Online Subscription Name:

User Name:

Password:

Online Subscription Name:

User Name:

Password:

Online Subscription Name:

User Name:

Password:

MEMBERSHIPS (CLUBS, GYM, RELIGIOUS, ETC)

Organization Name:

Phone #:

Organization Name:

Phone #:

Organization Name:

Phone #:

Organization Name:

Phone #:

Organization Name:

Phone #:

Organization Name:

Phone #:

Login Names and Passwords

CELL PHONE LOGIN

User Name:

Password:

Answer to Security Question:

COMPUTER LOGIN

User Name:

Password:

Answer to Security Question:

COMPUTER LOGIN

User Name:

Password:

Answer to Security Question:

TABLET LOGIN

User Name:

Password:

Answer to Security Question:

Email & Social Media

User Names and Passwords

EMAIL

Email Address/Service Provider:

User Name:

Password:

Email Address/Service Provider:

User Name:

Password:

Email Address/Service Provider:

User Name:

Password:

CLOUD ACCOUNT

User Name:

Password:

User Name:

Password:

SOCIAL MEDIA

Facebook:

User Name:

Password:

Facebook:

User Name:

Password:

LinkedIn:

User Name:

Password:

Instagram:

User Name:

Password:

Instagram:

User Name:

Password:

Skype:

User Name:

Password:

WhatsApp:

User Name:

Password:

Twitter:

User Name:

Password:

Other:

User Name:

Password:

Other:

User Name:

Password:

Other: ____

User Name: ____

Password: ____

____

Other: ____

User Name: ____

Password: ____

____

WEBSITE INFORMATION

Web Address: ____

User Name: ____

Password: ____

Hosting Service: ____

Phone #: ____

____

Web Address: ____

User Name: ____

Password: ____

Hosting Service: ____

Phone #: ____

Business Information

My Business Name:

Address:

Phone #:

Key Person (Payroll or Other):

Phone #:

Cell Phone #:

Landlord:

Address:

Phone #:

Accountant:

Company Name:

Address:

Phone #:

Attorney:

Company Name:

Address:

Phone #:

Bank:

Bank Name:

Address:

Contact Name:

Phone #:

Business Credit Card Information:

Mastercard ☐   Visa ☐   AmEx ☐   Discover ☐   Other ☐

Account #:   Phone #:

Online User Name: Password:

Expiration Date: CV Code #:

Business Credit Card Information: ___________________________

Mastercard ☐   Visa ☐   AmEx ☐   Discover ☐   Other ☐

Account #: _______________________   Phone #: _______________________

Online User Name: _________________   Password: _______________________

Expiration Date: __________________   CV Code #: _______________________

Business Related Insurance Companies: _______________________

(Property, Casualty, Benefits, Life & Health): _______________________

Primary Agent Name: _______________________

Phone #: _______________________

Address: _______________________

Primary Agent Name: _______________________

Phone #: _______________________

Address: _______________________

Location of Key Business Legal Documents, Royalties & Agreements: _______________________

Location of Business Formation Document: _______________________

Location of Buy/Sell Agreement:

____

Location of Key Person Agreement:

____

Location of Deferred Compensation Agreement:

____

Location of Severance Pay Agreement:

____

WEBSITE OR BLOG

Web Address:

User Name:

Password:

Hosting Service:

Phone #:

Web Master:

Phone #:

____

Blog User Name:

Password:

____

BUSINESS SOCIAL MEDIA SITES

Name:

User Name:

Password:

Name:

User Name:

Password:

Name:

User Name:

Password:

Name:

User Name:

Password:

www.ingramcontent.com/pod-product-compliance
Lightning Source LLC
Chambersburg PA
CBHW041353050726
47599CB00017B/1870